THE
SPACE
LESS
TRAVELED

STRAIGHT TALK FROM
APOLLO 14 ASTRONAUT
EDGAR MITCHELL

COMPILED BY CAROL MERSCH

PEN-L PUBLISHING

Pen-L

The Space Less Traveled: Straight Talk From
Apollo 14 Astronaut Edgar Mitchell
Compiled by Carol Mersch

First Edition October 2012
ISBN: 978-0-9851274-2-8

Published by
Pen-L Publishing
12 West Dickson #4455
Fayetteville, AR 72702

Visit our web site at www.Pen-L.com

This book was compiled in celebration of the 40th anniversary of the Institute of Noetic Sciences (IONS), an organization founded by Dr. Edgar Mitchell in 1972 to pursue the exploration of consciousness, sustainability, and the inherent power within each of us to make a difference.

In loving memory of Adam Mitchell

1984-2010

Table of Contents

"There is a saying in the world of public communications that if you can't dazzle them with brilliance, baffle them with bullshit. Since I can do neither, I will attempt to be articulate."

Dr. Edgar Mitchell
When Foxes Guard the Hen House

Introduction

On January 31, 1971, Navy Captain Dr. Edgar Mitchell embarked on a journey into outer space, resulting in his becoming the sixth man to walk on the Moon. The Apollo 14 mission was NASA's third manned lunar landing. This historic journey ended safely nine days later on February 9, 1971. It was an audacious time in the history of mankind. For Mitchell, however, the most extraordinary journey was yet to come.

As he hurtled earthward through the abyss between the two worlds, Mitchell became engulfed by a profound sensation—a sense of universal connectedness. He intuitively sensed that his presence, that of his fellow astronauts, and that of the planet in the window were all part of a deliberate universal process—and that the glittering cosmos itself was in some sense conscious. The experience was so overwhelming, that Mitchell knew his life would never be the same: "You don't look at our little planet from that perspective without its having a profound impact on your thinking."

And while Mitchell regarded his experience, his education, and his lunar endeavors as invaluable milestones, they would become mere stepping stones to what would eventually become his true life passion—exploring the power of the conscious mind. It is a subject he embraces passionately once one gets past the predictable discussions of his spaceflight experience.

The palpable presence of collective mind, ever present and ever at work in the universe, is something he is sure of and something he feels bears examination, not only in the euphoric musings of mystics, zealots, and dreamers, but in the harsh light of science. When Mitchell left NASA, it was to devote his life to the area he believed society had overlooked—man's potential, particularly the power of the mind.

In 1973 Mitchell founded the Institute of Noetic Sciences, an organization dedicated to exploring the underlying principles of consciousness in nature and how to apply this knowledge to the sustainability of our fragile spinning planet, spaceship Earth.

When Mitchell talks about these things, he loses the shyness and stiffness he takes on with strangers. He is not an easy person to get to know. Still, start Mitchell talking about planet Earth and the role of its inhabitants, and there is passion in his voice and the thoughts come tumbling out. He likes this role of maverick, explorer, forger of new frontiers.

This is what Mitchell wants to be remembered for. Yes, it's nice to be known as one of the twelve men who stood on the moon and looked back at Earth. But what Edgar Mitchell considers his major contribution is helping to transform the whole way we think about ourselves and our capabilities.

And he's not finished yet.

~ Carol Mersch

Perspective of a Moonwalker

"Although I have recorded the story of Apollo 14 and my impressions of that flight elsewhere, there is a particular experience that occurred on the flight that I think is worthy of a separate telling. It is a story all its own. It is the story of the powerful emotional experience I had in space as I looked upon the beauty of our planet as it appears in the cosmos.

Imagine the Earth, moon, and sun on plane. We are flying in 'barbeque mode' perpendicular to the elliptic plane and rotating in order to maintain a thermal balance. As we rotate every two minutes, I can see the Earth, the sun, the moon, the stars, the galaxies coming in parade across the window.

During my doctoral studies at MIT and Harvard I had studied about astronomy, star formation, and galactic formations, so I presumably knew how matter on Earth and the universe were formed in the furnace of those ancient stars. But I suddenly realized on the way home from the moon as I looked out at this, that the molecules of my body and the molecules of the spacecraft and my partners had been prototyped in some ancient generation of stars. That's good astrophysical theory—but suddenly those were *my* molecules. It wasn't an intellectual exercise anymore.

There was a sense of oneness, a connectedness that was very personal. What were my molecules doing out there? The sense of unity was overwhelming. It was staggering. I realized that our story of ourselves—who are we and how we got here—needed to be asked anew from the perspective of the first generation to travel into space.

Any questions that my curious mind might have had about our progress, about our destiny, about the nature of the universe, suddenly melted away as I experienced that oneness. I could reach out and touch the farthest parts and experience the vast reaches of the universe. It was clear that those tiny pinpoints of light in brilliant profusion were a part of the plan. They were linked together as part of the whole as they framed and formed a backdrop for this fragile planet Earth. I knew then that we were not alone in this universe—that earth was only one of millions, perhaps billions of planets like our own with intelligent life, all playing a role in that great divine plan in the evolution of life.

In an instant I knew for certain that what I was seeing

was no accident, that it did not occur randomly and without a plan, and that life did not, by accident, arise from the primordial earthly sea.

The story of ourselves as created from a scientific cosmology is incomplete and possibly flawed. And the story of ourselves as created by our cultural cosmologies is archaic and most certainly flawed.

The universe is interconnected in a way that we've never thought about before. It took me many months after that experience to understand what took place. This was a jarring awakening experience—a life-changing moment that could not be ignored."

~ Apollo 14 Astronaut Edgar Mitchell
The View from Space

THE

SPACE

LESS

TRAVELED

"Suddenly from behind the rim of the moon, long, slow-motion moments of immense majesty, there emerges a sparkling blue and white jewel, a light, delicate sky blue sphere, laced with slow swirling veils of white, rising gradually like a small pearl in a thick sea of black mystery. It takes more than a moment to fully realize this is Earth—home."

The Way of the Explorer

EARTH

The Space Less Traveled

"I have the home planet out the hatch window and it's passing very low. We only have a few moments in each window, but it's a most inviting and magnificent view. I'm very glad that we have the Earth as a home planet. I hope that we can keep it so inviting."

Reporting to Mission Control from Apollo 14
February 3, 1971

Earth

"It is quite apparent in the view from space how tiny, how fragile, how limited the Earth is if required to support a civilization determined to destroy itself by the misuse of its greatest gifts."

The View from Space

"We humans must learn to transcend our greed
and self service in order to serve the greater good
for all living creatures on this planet. It means we
learn to realize, at individual and societal levels,
that we are all interconnected and thus what we do
to one, we do to all—and to ourselves."

IONS Summary Report
October 23, 2008

Earth

"The issue is not just about saving nature—it's about saving *us*.

"It's not pay now or pay later. Its pay now or there will be no later."

"Toward a Sustainable Global Future"
IONS 2009

"An image of the Earth for those of us who have been in space evokes a sense of unity, because when you see Earth from space you don't see the disharmony, you don't see the boundaries, you see a unified magnificent beautiful planet that is our home. And only when you've been down here and realize how we humans fight and squabble and tear things up and destroy the environment and are insensitive to what we do, does it hit you pretty hard.

"We need to see it and understand it from the point of view of what it looks like when you're out and away from Earth. It looks harmonious, unified, and consistent, and without boundaries—but we don't live that way."

Documentary: "Voices for Sustainability"
Living Dreams Films, 2010

Earth

"We now possess the power and knowledge to control Earth, but do we yet have the wisdom and sense of destiny necessary to control the technological genie we have set free? Has the lid to Pandora's Box been opened ever so little? Has the sorcerer's apprentice opened the great book of magic?"

The View from Space

"As humans, we all think our thoughts, dream our dreams, of a better and peaceful place to live. But thoughts, dreams, and visions alone do not change the world."

The View from Space

Earth

"For Earth to survive as a planet and to provide for the nurturing, the growth, and well-being of its inhabitants, then we, humankind, must rise to the challenge of learning to be stewards to the planet and to each other."

The View from Space

"Unrestrained exponential growth in any closed system is not sustainable. It cannot be sustained indefinitely on a finite space."

"Toward a Sustainable Global Future"
IONS 2009

"We are the crew of spaceship Earth and we are in mutiny. And how can you run a spaceship with a crew that is mutinous?"

"A Voyage into Mind and Space"
Chicago Planetary Studies Foundation, March 2004

"The United States is the largest energy-
consuming country on Earth—and with no
comprehensive energy strategy."

"Toward a Sustainable Global Future"
IONS 2009

Earth

"It is time we concentrate on leaving this planet in
a little better shape than it was when we arrived."

Albuquerque Journal
March 30, 1971

"The journey to the moon was a very powerful experience; it was life changing. We have been saying since the early days of the Apollo program that if we could ever get our political leaders to have a summit meeting in space, we'd have a totally different world."

San Francisco Chronicle
September 16, 2007

"Civilization needs to give a great deal of thought
to exactly what it's doing to itself."

Response to a visitor
Spacefest Conference, Phoenix, AZ
August 2007

"We have within us the seeds to create ourselves as a harmonious, kind, and loving crew of spaceship Earth. But we have missed the message."

"A Voyage into Mind and Space"
Chicago Planetary Studies Foundation
March 2004

Earth

Excerpt from exchange between Edgar Mitchell and India's revered Sadhguru, founder of the Isha Foundation, a profound mystic, a visionary humanitarian, and a prominent spiritual leader.

Sadhguru: Food is the raw material. What you call a body is a heap of cauliflower. Before we came to this planet, a boundless number of people walked this planet. Where are they? They're topsoil! We will also be topsoil one day.

Mitchell: Okay, we're getting closer together.

Sadhguru: We've never been far apart.

Mitchell: But there has got to be more meaning to life than just topsoil!

Sadhguru: So there is something in you that is capable of making a cauliflower into a human being. This is not a small thing. It is a phenomenon!

IONS Conference, Tucson, AZ
June 2009

MANKIND

Mankind

"We are universal beings. We are stewards and keepers of spaceship Earth, not the spoiled, self-serving brats we portray, a species not knowing our own potential, not sensing the omnipotence of God or the limitlessness of our creative capability. Not recognizing our God-given gifts of intelligence, intuition, creativity—that the spirit within us is the guiding force that makes mankind great. It enables us to rise above our more base instincts to become the creative, intelligent, loving creatures of the universe that is our true reality."

The View from Space

"We can find false prophets, we can find false leaders, and we can lead ourselves down false paths. But eventually, if we're open, we find our way back to something that is testable, true, and valid."

"Heroes and Healers"
November 2002

Mankind

"A mind change is required in order to change our value system to values that are important. And transcendence is vital. And getting past ego is vital. You've heard me say, and certainly others have said, that this is the basis of religion. And until we understand our connectedness and are willing to live a life of service, as opposed to a life of ego, we're not there. Until we understand that we are all interconnected—and we either hang together or separately—we haven't got the message yet."

Interview by Carol Mersch
2005

"The human is not just an intelligent animal, born to struggle for survival, needing to defend its territory against all intruders, but a limitless spiritual creature, having a body with which to achieve its goals of learning and perfection. The picture of mankind painted by the scientists of medicine, biology, chemistry and traditional psychology, only describes our fragile physical machine. Not our essence. Not our basic immortal nature."

The View from Space

Mankind

"One damning distinction between human and animal culture is that the human leaves a trail of useless debris wherever he wanders."

When Foxes Guard the Hen House

"The past will not suffice to govern the future, for the past is wrapped in ignorance and false beliefs about what is, however well the beliefs served their times at the time."

Albuquerque Journal
March 30, 1971

Mankind

"Many realities exist simultaneously, as many as there are humans to interpret what reality is. For it is the individual interpretation of reality, or "world view," not objective reality itself, that guides human decisions. Objective reality is but an illusive idealization to be sought and approximated but never really known. It is why the authors use the word 'reality' and 'game' almost interchangeably. Because the mind interprets its own version of reality, we continuously rediscover our prejudices and reinforce them. But we can change our minds. We can choose. Confrontation or cooperation is a matter of choice."

When Foxes Guard the Hen House

The Space Less Traveled

"The space experience makes one know, without
doubt, that there is a divine direction and purpose
in the universe. It is sad to realize that mankind has
reached the point where he essentially has control
over all the elements, yet he has not learned to live
with himself or his neighbors."

The Sunday Brand , Hereford, TX
Sept 2, 1971

Mankind

"We have tremendous technological genius; it's too bad our knowledge of ourselves and how to live together has not progressed commensurately."

The Sunday Brand, Hereford, TX
Sunday September 2, 1971

"Traditional human viewpoints existing for centuries, revered and hallowed, lead us into dangerous waters as we look to the past for answers that should come from the present."

When Foxes Guard the Henhouse

Mankind

"Why are we here? What is our purpose? Are we simply a step above the animals? Are the planets and stars really formed by the random and accidental collision of matter, coming together in space because of gravitation? Is it really all an accident? Or is there much, much more?"

The View from Space

"What has been our greatest excuse for war over the centuries has been religious differences, how we justify our conquest, our terrorism, our violence, our preying upon other human beings and nature by using a religious argument 'because my God is better than yours, my viewpoint is better than yours.' And we go around killing each other in the name of religion."

Interview by Carol Mersch
2006

Mankind

"The technology of civilization has totally
outstripped its morality."

Interview by Carol Mersch
2005

"We ignore that inner voice—hearing what we want to hear, seeing what we want to see—to satisfy the desires of the moment. We believe that life is hard, the environment threatening, and thus have made it so."

The View from Space

Search

Life's been a very curious road.
The twists and turns are legion.
It's led me up the highest mount
And wound through every season.

It's held the hope that soon enough
I'd find that dream-come-true,
By plunging ever forward
Along a path that's new.

But each new path I've followed,
With hopes so high and bright,
Has turned into another,
That goes on out of sight.

I followed 'long each pathway,
To choose the best I can,
At each and every crossing
A branch that met my plan

To find the great Tomorrow
Where all the wants are met.
I've searched and hoped, dreamt, and chose,
But haven't found it yet.

The Space Less Traveled

The secret is to plan and dream.
To walk life's paths, you see.
But the glory that each searches for
Is right here in you and me.

Nature lets us seek our way
To find what's to behold,
But smugly keeps the secret
That will for each unfold.

The key to life is deep inside
The mind and heart of each.
For love, life, and beauty
That's all there is to teach.

Along the path each learns the truth
That the goal's not ahead of me.
For all along its wondrous route
As we learn to love, we see.

From a collection of poems by Edgar Mitchell

Mankind

"It is in us to turn the course of mankind into a gentler and more abundant civilization. If not us—who? If not now—when?"

Lecture, Unity Church, Germantown, TN
January 23, 2005

SELF

Self

"Blessings often arrive unannounced. Sometimes they come disguised as misfortune."

The Way of the Explorer

"We often say, 'seeing is believing'—but precisely the opposite is true. Believing is seeing. When we change our belief, we will see ourselves differently."

Interview by Carol Mersch
2003

"We function like 12-cylinder engines operating on only one cylinder because we do not know what we are. This inefficient operation is only because we do not recognize that we have other great potentials. We are limited only because we think we are limited."

The View from Space

"As tiny as our physical bodies are on the scale of the universe, our minds can reach out to become one with all that is."

The View from Space

Self

"We can continue to think narrowly, selfishly, and seeing only that limited view of ourselves. Or we can set about changing our belief, and thus change what we see—begin to see ourselves in a more expansive magnificent role. But the choice is ours individually, and no one can do it for us. It is ours, each and every one. For only as we change our belief about ourselves and our belief about our reality will we start to see what we can become."

The View from Space

The Space Less Traveled

"We are limited even in the body only by what we believe about ourselves."

The View from Space

Self

"It helps us to know that we are not the victims of the world and victims of our circumstances. But indeed, if victims at all, we are victims of our own thinking."

The View from Space

"What is it that we could become if we would dare?"

The View from Space

"Where intuition, emotion, and intellect come together, they can almost preserve you. It takes instinct to navigate the course of life."

Interview by Carol Mersch
2003

"The important lesson is that the only thing we can really change is ourselves."

Interview by C. L. Mersch
2005

Self

"Each choice we make branches the universe into the many probabilities available. The one we find ourselves in corresponds to the choice we made."

The Way of the Explorer

Essence

Daylight and darkness are part of each life
As is joy, followed then by despair.
As seasons of life bring warmth, then the ice,
Days seem gloomy, then fair.

Travail brings on learning, of that I am sure,
Its purpose to set us aright.
How can one have the joy of a glorious day
Unless compared to the night?

To dwell only in sunlight seems wondrous indeed,
But even great wonders grow cold.
To the restless heart not tested with strife,
Without meter to measure the mold.

Let go of all fear, it's but a shadow held near,
It creates all stridence and stress.
Its place will be filled by a love that is willed
To bring light for your happiness.

That love's all around, its nature unbound.
The essence of life when we're free
From the fears we create, with our anger and hate,
It's our natural self don't you see.

Self

The choices we make, each moment awake
Determine the rules of the game
So make love the choice, heed the small inner
voice
That says: "Life, love and joy are the same."

Excerpt from a collection of poems by Edgar Mitchell

"Trust the process. With faith and perseverance
the means will always come together so that we can
take the next step."

The Way of the Explorer

Self

"Disbelief prevents one from seeing what one wishes not to."

The Way of the Explorer

"The fundamental thing...is giving meaning to experience. And if you give false meaning, or you give irrelevant meaning, or you give warped meaning to experience, that will affect your future decisions."

Interview by Carol Mersch
2003

.   "Our happiness and well being start inside—right
here, right now."

"Toward a Sustainable Global Future"
IONS 2009

"Anything that's set in motion physically has to be first set in motion mentally."

Interview with C. L. Mersch
2003

Self

"I don't upset my psyche over something I can't do anything about."

Interview by Carol Mersch
2003

"Our bodies respond to the diurnal cycles of energy and to our internal processes, including thought—not to the clock."

The Way of the Explorer

Self

"You need excitement to make any endeavor work. But if excitement is all you've got—you're in trouble."

Interview by C.L. Mersch
2005

Musing of a Father

Little boy at play
so innocent, so wise,
the playmates that you see
unseen by other eyes.
Tell me what you feel today
before this world so rude
intrudes and makes its madness
a place not understood.

When you're young
and filled with awe,
you communicate with gods.
Our rushed adult existence
seems strange and all at odds.
Just wait, my son, ere long you'll see,
time will force, upon your mind
a new reality.

We'll make you think like we do
in order to survive
for life here does not honor
those with views so wide.

Self

You'll put away your pixies
and the little folk you see
they're not a part of this life
called adult reality.

They're from another realm of life
just as real as this,
where doubts of things don't enter in
to form the great abyss
between the things that matter forms
and the things of mind.
Adults close off the doorway
to pictures of that kind.

Only when you're older and have tried the other way
perhaps the thought will come to you
of what I've said today.
Wisdom comes with knowing, both within and
from without
How to pull it all together and live without a doubt
That what you know within you
is right and strong and free
Wisdom honors nature and all life like you and me.

The Space Less Traveled

Life can be so barren, when all there is to see
are the things made out of matter
called adult reality.
Then you'll search for wisdom beyond the great
abyss
where mind flows into matter
but gently as a kiss.

But in this world that we have made
such thoughts are often lost.
They are drowned out by the clatter
of wins at any cost.
Just keep your dreams and wishes
alive where ere you can
Resist the compromises that diminish any man.

Hold to that inner wisdom,
Because it's pure and true
It will make life's Earthly journey full of love
and joy for you.

From a collection of poems by Edgar Mitchell
(projecting his own youth on his step-son, Paul)

SPIRITUALITY

"While orbiting the moon awaiting reentry into the trajectory back to Earth, the slow spin of the capsule brought into my view through the small window a celestial rotation of spheres—the Earth, the moon, the milky way—and a sudden and palpable sense of universal harmony. I was struck with the overwhelming reality that the universe had a plan, had direction, had harmony, was structured and organized and moved with the thought of God, and not a lifeless, inanimate machine on which we are accidental passengers."

The Way of the Explorer

Spirituality

"We are connected to every species. We are connected to everything in the universe in a very powerful way. And when you merge into all that is, and there's nothing but awareness of all that is, this is a core experience—and this is the root of all religious experience."

'Heroes and Healers"
November 2002

"When we are able, either through circumstance or endeavor, to transcend, you realize your connectedness with everything. You realize that service is more vital and important to your own well being—and the well being of everyone—than self aggrandizement. And so it becomes less of an impulse to follow the trodden path.

"You always have the choice, but you no longer feel comfortable in it. You can't do it. It's not your nature any more. That has been the case for all of the transcendent masters, and there are more and more now. You don't have to be called a transcendent master like Jesus, you just have to take the path and follow it."

Interview by Carol Mersch
2006

"We must abandon the view of ourselves as provincial limited victims of life, accidents of evolution, and start to view ourselves as limitless creatures of God."

The View from Space

"I find it extraordinarily significant that [Albert] Einstein, the physicist, looking at the telescopic world of outer space, and [Sir John] Eccles, the neurophysiologist, looked at the microscopic world of inner space only to discover the same thing — the existence of God."

Psychic Exploration

Spirituality

"To me, spirituality is the pursuit of truth. And unless you can validate that truth in some profound way, and live by it, then you haven't found it."

Interview by Carol Mersch
2003

"There are no natural or supernatural phenomena, only very large gaps in our knowledge of what is natural. We should strive to fill those gaps of ignorance."

The Way of the Explorer

Spirituality

"Whoever said the age of miracles passed long ago hasn't been paying attention."

The Way of the Explorer

The Space Less Traveled

"That there is purpose—that there is order and harmony in the universe—changes the entire way that we think about ourselves."

The View from Space

Spirituality

"Looking back on these times, I see how naïve I was. For several years I would continue to underestimate the power of belief in our lives because of the pervasiveness of my classical scientific training."

The Way of the Explorer

"Nature doesn't waste experience."

Lecture at Unity Church
Dallas, TX, March 2006
when asked about life after death

Spirituality

"Spirituality is the *pursuit*. It's a way of being—on the path, seeking—not knowing the answers but refusing to accept the religious dogma."

Interview by Carol Mersch
2003

"I believe in a divine creation, in the idea that the universe is constructed in this marvelous way that allows these mysterious processes that we experience, but can't, with our earlier knowledge be very definitive about. And of course if we're really seekers, we're looking for definitive knowledge. And some people say it doesn't matter if you know what it is. Well, if you're going to use it, yes, you need to know what it is."

Lecture at Whitehouse High School, Germantown, TN
January 2005
(when asked if he believed in God)

"As a result of my experience in space, any doubt that I had about the Universe being a divine creation evaporated, to be replaced with the certainty that the physical Universe and its creatures are the result of divine thought and purpose. I view the spiritual aspect of life as the most important part of human experience and believe that growth in the spiritual dimensions is limited only by our individual unwillingness to see beyond our fears and selfish interests.

"To seek tranquility and joy by realizing one's true spiritual nature is the ultimate goal of all life."

In a letter to Apollo 15 Astronaut Jim Irwin
August 23, 1978

"How do you tell religion from spirituality? That's where I think science comes in. Deeply we are spiritual creatures, recognizing something beyond physicality. The transcendent experience is an inner emotional experience. And I think it is built right into our nature. If the postulate I make here is correct, the transcendent experience represents ground state quantum resonance with the 'zero-point' energy field, which is the ground of all being. This ground of all being in any other term you could call God, but it is the essence, the clay, from which we are molded. And it contains all the possibilities of the physicality of our universe, otherwise they wouldn't exist."

Interview by Carol Mersch
2003

"I am reminded of an ancient verse that serves me well when I lose a perspective of our higher nature, for it describes the reality I want to see. It was originally written in Sanskrit and goes:

> *God sleeps in the minerals*
> *Awakens in the plants*
> *Walks in the animals*
> *And thinks in man."*

Lecture at Convention Center
Germantown, TN, January 23, 2005

LOVE

Love Means Letting Go of Fear

When we begin to add fear to our minds
Regardless of how it accrues,
We limit the places we are willing to go
And cut off our most joyous views.

The more fear we find on the map in our mind
Of what this life's all about
The less we love, the light dims above
Joy and laughter seem to go out.

But the game is not done, the course is not run
There's laughter ahead to be found.
When we see that our choice is to hear that small voice
Whose song melts the fears that abound.

The map in our mind has illusions not kind
That are made of shadows so bold.
We believe they are real, they do naught but conceal
The love that is ours to behold.

Our task, I believe, is to find we're deceived
When our mind says: "I am afraid."
The deceiver is me, it's my choice that I see
The shadows illusion has made.

The Space Less Traveled

I choose to live free of the fears that haunt me,
I no longer want them inside.
The map in my mind of what's real will now find
That love floods in like the tide.

From a collection of poems by Edgar Mitchell

Love

"It seemed to me that the missing link between the two models of reality, science on the one hand and our religious experience on the other, was the nature of consciousness. Thinking of myself as a scientist, but wanting to understand the enigma, I wanted to explore the commonality. The commonality is that all are rooted in the concept of love, and the concept of interconnectedness, and the concept of the human mind, and the spirit's ability to transcend all of that. This is the union of all that is."

"Heroes and Healers"
November 2002

Muffy's Graduation

My child so fair with angel's hair
Dancing eyes that look ahead, but with doubts
That your courage can hold for a future bold,
That your life will fill with lovers, not louts.

Your hopes O' so bright but with trembles at night
That your sunshine might turn into rain,
When the light of your life turns joy into strife
As he leaves to build castles in Spain.

You've grown in these years thru joy and tears,
Gained in wisdom and beauty besides.
Your little girl form has burst forth like a storm
To turn head and cause father to chide.

The eager young lad with a yarn oh so sad.
"Not with my girl, mind your manners, there, Sir.
The games you will play break hearts, not today,
I know, I was there once myself, Sir."

This growing up state, I was told by a sage
Will pass too – what a sigh of relief!
My hair's turning gray, the bills that I pay
Make me weak, but I hold tight the belief.

Love

That the race has been won, a new place in the sun
Awaits you, look eagerly ahead.
You make me so proud, I'll say it aloud
My Muffy's grown wise and well bred.

Her years here to learn cause me to yearn
To regain some years of my own.
Where words I have said just fill me with dread,
Where anger, not love, have I shown.

But today is your day
A new page in your life,
A day filled with joy and love.
No longer so wild, a woman, not child
go forward —you're blessed from above.

From a collection of poems by Edgar Mitchell
(written for his step-daughter, Mary Beth, in late 1970s)

The Roué's Downfall

My heart pounds at the nearness of you
It leaps at a caring word.
Lost feelings awake at the touch of your hand
Trite phrases are mouthed, quite absurd.

Where has gone the man, more erudite,
Never at loss for a phrase.
Clear thinking and strong, a master of fate
But suddenly lost in a maze.

Of feelings and stirrings, things long forgot
A man, now boy in a blink.
The years roll away as wonder returns
First loves are awakened, I think.

A little bit silly, a little bit bold
The giddy feel of a blush
The rush of desire, wanting to hold
Little brothers have said "what mush."

It seems so strange that one such as I
Would react this way to your charm
It's the female, you see, that gets weak at the knee
And tumbles right into my arms.

Love

But the tables are turned, the die is cast
Sweet fate has given reward
It is I that succumbs to your charms, my dear
It is you that moves love forward.

From a collection of poems by Edgar Mitchell

WAR

War

"If we want to heal the breach we have created in humanity, we're going to have to look beyond our differences and look at our similarities. And look at the fact that deep within us we have the capability to forgive. We have the capability to make peace with each other. But we have to want it very badly."

"Voyage into Mind and Space,"
Chicago Planetary Studies Foundation, March 2004

"World peace is an idea simple in principle but difficult to achieve in practice because, as individual members of our species, we have not found peace within ourselves. Societies cannot be peaceful societies until the members of the society look peacefully toward each other. But, it is impossible to look peacefully toward each other under constant threat for one's survival.

"Only when individuals take total responsibility for their own lives, find within themselves communion with the Creative Force, and live in peace with their neighbors and environment, only then will forces be set in motion that will eventually bring about world peace.

"We must be able to seek communion with our God without fear that individual beliefs will be ridiculed or oppressed by others.

(continued)

War

"No power can create peace when humans have fear, anger, and hate in their hearts, however insignificant those individual humans may think they are."

"Thoughts on World Peace"
Universal Peace Conference, 1983

"All strife, conflict, and terrorism arise from unfulfilled human need and greed, fueled by a healthy dose of expectation—and usually coupled with ignorance."

When Foxes Guard the Hen House

War

"As for military conflict, we're not dealing with a short-term process here, we're dealing with a long-term process. The real question is, can we do it quickly enough, soon enough to prevent us from destroying ourselves? There is a likelihood that any conflict like we are experiencing in the Mideast or that we are experiencing on our territory, if we're not very wise and very careful, can expand into a nuclear exchange. And eventually a nuclear exchange is going to reduce civilization as well."

The Monthly Aspectarian
November 2001

"Should we not be praying, not only for the world leaders, but for the terrorists as well? Of course we should. Put your intentionality there—that's what prayer is. When you're putting your intentionality out, that's powerful."

"The Future of Healing"
WLRN-TV, October 10, 2001

War

"If you go back in history and study the inner core of virtually all religions, they talk about brotherhood, harmony with nature, love for one another. That is a central message that has come down through the ages in perennial philosophy and in our religions. What we have tended to do is become radical, and forget the core, and get all tied up in our ego, and do unpleasant things to each other. That is what we need to correct.

"But it depends upon each one of us, regardless of our faith, to look at the deeper core that says, I am a human being, we are all human beings, and we are related to each other on this earth because we are all of the same cloth. And so are the animal species and other life that we share this planet with. It's up to us to recognize this, to live in harmony with it, and to promote the wellbeing of all life forms."

Lecture at Whitehouse High School, Germantown, TN
January 2005

"The veneer of our civilization is so thin that it can be shattered world wide by a single border dispute."

The View from Space

War

"Had Nature destined us to fly, it would provide wings, and to assault each other, the weapons. It did neither. We discovered how ourselves. And must therefore manage the consequences of our discoveries."

When Foxes Guard the Hen House

"It is we that must have the moral imperative, not the technology we develop."

"A Voyage Into Mind and Space,"
Chicago Planetary Studies Foundation, March 2004

War

"Whether it's a good application or bad application
depends on the morality of the people applying it."

Interview with Carol Mersch
2005

"The most dangerous type of war is when the warrior need not look into the eyes of his victim."

When Foxes Guard the Hen House

War

"One of the pervasive traditions of human behavior is the veneration of conquest and war as a necessity of existence. However, traditional and instinctive as it may be, much conventional wisdom resists such a fundamental change, it is a human activity that must be outgrown and left behind if the species of Earth—all species—are to survive. But it is not a behavior that will be changed quickly nor easily. Evolution has never worked its wonders rapidly.

"But change it must, for there is no other way to exist as populations crowd the Earth and destructive technologies increase their power. Many species of this planet have disappeared as they failed to adapt to changing conditions. The time has come for Homo sapiens to confront that eventuality.

"Fortunately, unlike our neighbors in the animal kingdom, we have a wide freedom of choice. We

(*continued*)

have created the very conditions that now threaten us. And what has been chosen and created badly, can be changed by the enlightened choice of we who have done the creating."

When Foxes Guard the Hen House

War

"When my time came and I had finished my obligated service, and I wasn't going to get to fly in space anymore, I was ready to get out. I wanted loose from the military game. It had brought me rewards, it had brought me acclaim and satisfaction, things I had never dreamed of to begin with. But I no longer needed to carry the mantle of a warrior—a peaceful warrior maybe, but not with weapons."

Interview by Carol Mersch
2003

"When foxes guard the henhouse someone must watch the foxes, else only they are satisfied."

When Foxes Guard the Hen House

War

"Human excesses and error have historically sorted themselves out in the fullness of the centuries. But never before has the capacity existed for humans to terminate all living activity on the planet in one spasmodic hour of nuclear exchange."

When Foxes Guard the Hen House

"Regardless of what one does with the new technologies, while playing under the old rules everyone loses. That result requires some new and deep¯ thought. There is a prophetic quote at the end of the cinema *War Games*: 'The only way to win is not to play."

When Foxes Guard the Henhouse

War

"The Administration and the Department of
Defense press on undeterred toward development
and deployment of a system which they yet hope
can meet some scaled down version of the nuclear
weaponization of space. They seem to enunciate,
like a 'snake oil' salesman, whatever justification
seems plausible and saleable to the audience of
the moment. A 'don't confuse me with facts'
scenario is being acted out on an international
stage before the eyes of the world. This can only
become more embarrassing and a damage to
American credibility should it continue . . . The
weak links of the concept and program will
eventually break, but will the victim be the
American people?"

When Foxes Guard the Henhouse
Regarding proposed Strategic Defense Initiative (SDI)

"Modern humans who prize freedom, human rights, and equality, cannot equate defense with offense except as a measure of last resort."

When Foxes Guard the Henhouse

War

"For the first time in history, the people's leaders are less at risk than the people during a war. This is a significant fact. It is a fact which dictates in part the necessity for new 'rules of the game' in the modern era of missile and space warfare: to compute separately the probable outcomes of war for the populations and their champions since they are no longer the same for the two groups. A leader's win does not assure that his population has won also."

When Foxes Guard the Henhouse

"If the defender, in defense of his territory, launches a pre-emptive first strike, is he still a defender? Is one's defense of moral righteousness still righteous if all existence is threatened? Or does it really matter what one calls it? By whatever one calls it, a rose is still a rose and Armageddon is still a war of annihilation. The first needs no explanation and smells just as sweet; the second cannot be explained if no one remains to hear."

When Foxes Guard the Henhouse

"It would seem that an in-depth knowledge of psychology would be more important for a Secretary of Defense than knowledge of military technology."

When Foxes Guard the Henhouse

"I once was confronted by a man with homicidal intentions. Looking at his eyes, I discovered he was more frightened than I."

When Foxes Guard the Henhouse

War

"I was a test pilot and naval aviator trained in carrier landings toward the end of the Korean War. But the Korean War was over. We were a peace-keeping force. There were political tensions in the Cold War between the Communist world and our world. My attitude even from the earliest days was that I didn't believe in war as a solution to anything; and I kept hoping that someday my profession would be obsolete—being a warrior. And that we had to get past that. That was my thinking. I was going in because my country demanded it, the draft was on, and I had to do it. So in keeping with the family training and tradition, even with discretion, I said, okay, this is a reality, make the best of it.

"It's not a perfect world we live in, we could make it better. And that's another thing I considered about our world, that we should be ready to evolve out of war games. Particularly since in that era we were carrying nuclear weapons. That put emphasis

(continued)

on it, because from my early days, not only in
P2V's but in A-3's, we had nuclear training for the
weapons we carried. It was pretty obvious, from
Hiroshima in WWII, that if we ever really began
using nuclear weapons, civilization as we knew it
was at an end. So we are going to have to learn to
handle civilization in a totally different way. And I
recognized that from my earliest days.

"I was a good pilot. My bombardiers could always
hit the target. And if that's what we had to do,
that's what we did. But I prayed we'd never have to
do that."

Interview by Carol Mersch
2005

SUSTAINABILITY

"We're consuming ourselves out of house and home, and we don't have too long to get things squared away. The global warming phenomenon is real. We are doing ourselves in by consumption and rapid growth of population. We need to know how to get along better with each other and solve these types of problems as a civilization, not as just a few individuals yelling about it."

Interview by Rob Sidon
Common Ground, May 2012

"The record in Genesis 1, verse 17, states: '---be fruitful, multiply.' Now, if after the word 'multiply,' had Adam's mind not been focused well below his belt buckle, he would have recognized that 'be fruitful' also means 'be productive.' And that 'replenish the earth' (little 'e') isn't the same as 're-populate the Earth' (big 'E'). No, 'replenish the earth' (little 'e') means to put back into the earth what you take out of it—that is to say, recycle and nourish the earth....and 'dominion over' also means to be 'responsible for.'

"So, if Adam hadn't been having a severe libido attack when the orders were handed out, the instructions might likely have been understood and passed on down to us in the following way: 'Work hard and be productive, multiply, replace, and nourish that which you take from the earth; tame it and make it more hospitable with love and kindness; and be responsible for the wellbeing of

(*continued*)

the fish of the sea, the fowl of the air, and for every living thing that moveth upon the earth.'

"And correcting that initial error is what sustainability is all about."

Excerpt from his paper
"Go Forth and Sustain the World," 1996

Sustainability

"We no longer can follow the patterns of our
earlier more primitive infantile years on Earth,
patterns of the generations before who believed,
because we were few in number and the Earth was
so large, that its resources would last forever—
believed, and still believe—that conquest creates
conformity and threat produces peace."

The View from Space

"My vision is that the third millennium will bring a new dawn of awareness such that the genius and creativity which we exhibit as individuals will be harnessed together in concert, globally, to resolve the problems which we have unwittingly collectively created and which threaten existence as we know it.

"This vision cannot possibly become reality without each of us, as he or she awakens to the dilemma, to first make a personal decision to live life productively toward creating a sustainable civilization for all, then to reach beyond our personal commitment to self and family to assist others also to recognize that our cultural traditions have created the crisis and must be re-examined."

> "My Vision for the Third Millennium"
> paper by Edgar Mitchell

Sustainability

"We need less fuel and more feet."

"Toward a Sustainable Global Future"

"The wonders of technological and economic progress in this century and the global crises which that progress has also produced are well documented in hundreds of learned papers, books and video accounts.

"The difficult questions that remain are: How do we persuade the most technologically and economically advanced individuals, corporations and nations that the economic strategy of promoting unlimited growth and increased levels of consumption is leading to disaster for all?

"How do we persuade the less technologically and economically advanced individuals, enterprises and nations not to follow the lead of those who are currently more financially successful, but rather to search for sustainable alternatives?

"And how do we persuade the largest group of all, those who are undereducated and poor, that they also must contribute to the solution by curbing

(continued)

population growth and to nourish the earth rather
than continuing to ravage its abundance to the
detriment of future generations?"

"My Vision for the Third Millennium"

The Space Less Traveled

"Technologically we are ready to explore the cosmos. Economically we are mostly devoted to greed. Educationally we are still largely illiterate. Culturally we are parochial and divisive. Spiritually few know their own soul, having entrusted it to traditional dogmas. My vision, indeed, my article of faith for the opening of the new millennium, is that we can and will evolve consciously and quickly to transcend these limitations of our juvenile species and attain the mature and glorious adulthood of world stewardship."

"My Vision for the Third Millennium"

Earth

O' puny race of men, vainglorious and puffed up,
why destroy you the Mother
who alone among the stars
has given life?

Who, nurturing her spawn,
siblings in all forms,
allows each to find its way
without reproach.

Wherein lies the truth that men seek to find
to guide their way?
In the stars or in the earth?
Or in the Self, which seeks to know
to calm its strife?

Peace that knows no end is hidden within,
while men search the answer without.
Assured that in their play
with fire, the answers lurk.

To err is death to all, the fire consuming
the Mother too, who protests not
the senior sibling's folly,
until the end, giving what there is.

When Foxes Guard the Henhouse

"When all the trees have been cut down,
When all the animals have been hunted,
When all the waters are polluted,
When all the air is unsafe to breathe,
Only then will you discover that you cannot eat,
drink, or breathe money."

Edgar Mitchell, IONS, July 2009
quoting from a Cree prophecy

QUANTUM ENTANGLEMENT

"Thoughts are powerful intentional things that create physical results in the world. Our intentionality has an effect. To a certain extent we create a reality by the way we think about it. We create our personal reality by the way we react to it."

Lecture at Whitehouse High School, Germantown, TN
January 2005

"We need to develop a constant conscious 'listening' to the invisible signs and forces, to the echoes of life, both here and in distant places and time—perhaps the future."

Lecture at Unity Church
Dallas, TX 2006

Quantum Entanglement

"In the English language we call our intuition our sixth sense, but we really ought to call it our first sense because it's rooted in the quantum properties of nature. It was around long before our sun was around, our planet, and us. Having studied this, I'm convinced that the animal kingdom communicates directly through these quantum resonances."

UACC Conference, San Antonio, TX
August 2006

"One of the problems of science is a holdover of classical days in which time the Newtonian classical universe was thought to be an absolute of the universe, therefore time had reality. In the quantum hologram model, only *process* has reality. And the most important processes, those that are far from equilibrium and non-linear, only move in one direction—toward the future."

'Heroes and Healers"
November 2002

"What I lacked in my early years was an understanding of how intuition, emotion, and intellect interrelate. . . I didn't yet fully understand that at the bottom of all matter there was no single coherent picture of physical reality."

The Way of the Explorer

"One of the things we are learning is that your belief system biases an experiment. If you believe certain results will take place and a colleague in Europe doesn't think the results are valid, the same protocol with both will show that the one who thinks they will get positive results will get positive results. The one who thinks they won't get positive results, won't get positive results. These results were replicated several times to show how our belief about things shapes the outcome of the things we do. That is because our intentionality has an effect."

Interview by Carol Mersch
2003

"There is a hidden observer within each of us that exists separate from our experience of physical reality."

The Way of the Explorer

"To a certain extent, we create reality by the way we think about it. And certainly it is obvious that we create our own reality by the way we react to whatever situation we find ourselves in. So this role of mind in shaping reality is becoming very well established. And we need to learn this, because you get yourself into a lot of trouble just because you think in certain ways. And you get yourself into making choices that are not appropriate choices."

Lecture at Whitehouse High School, Germantown, TN
January 2005

Quantum Entanglement

"There is a vital word, called 'non-locality.' It means you cannot shield the effect. You can shield light, but you can't shield gravity. And you can't shield quantum entanglement."

Lecture at Whitehouse High School, Germantown, TN
January 2005

"In noetics, it is the experience of the mental perception that is important—*that* is the reality. The matter world that we live in and that we've been trained in, that's the matter world only because we perceive it that way."

For All Mankind

Quantum Entanglement

"What happens to one happens to all."

'Heroes and Healers"
November 2002

"It is obvious that we live in an interactive system, a participatory system where our thoughts and behaviors interact and influence the physical world around us. So we're co-creators in a sense of our own success and failures."

Interview by Carol Mersch
2003

Question: Please tell us more about the ESP/telepathy experiments that were conducted from the lunar surface.

"It was done in lunar orbit between the moon and the earth. It was conducted exactly the same as had been done in laboratories and several parapsychology laboratories over the years. I simply used their protocol that had been done before. I had a knee pad with columns on it where I could randomize the numbers and symbols, so-called Zinner symbols, and order them randomly and think about it for 15 seconds. I then took them back [to Earth] and let the people on the ground that were receiving it at stated times send me their answers. I turned my thoughts and their data over to the experts, Dr. J. B. Rhine and Dr. Karlis Osis in NY, both of whom worked in the laboratory with these things continuously. And our results were just as good as they were getting in their laboratories, but ours taken from 150,000 to 240,000 miles away."

(continued)

The Space Less Traveled

Note: Mitchell collected the results of his private experiment and submitted them to Dr. Rhine at Duke University. At the Duke laboratory, Rhine's analysis pointed toward a positive result. Seeking verification, the participants sought a second analysis by Dr. Karlis Osis in New York, a well-known researcher in the field. Dr. Osis reported the statistics were such that there was only a one-in-three-thousand probability that the results were purely chance. The results reinforced Mitchell's scientific interest in the power of the conscious mind. - C. L. Mersch, *The Apostles of Apollo.*

Astronaut Scholarship Foundation *Astrogram*, May 2012
Online Astro Chat with Edgar Mitchell

Quantum Entanglement

"Randomness isn't random. It is simply noise in a collective mind."

Interview by Carol Mersch
2003

"If the power of intention can affect inanimate objects, then you would think it could also affect other people's actions."

Interview by Carol Mersch
2003

Quantum Entanglement

"Electromagnetic fields fall off as the inverse square of the distance."

Psychic Exploration

"In the field of quantum fluctuations, the great difficulty in classical theory is that forces are transmitted by things banging into each other, like billiard balls, where the force of two physical objects hitting each other is transferred along the chain. We know that as the temperature is reduced in matter, when we get to absolute zero, all molecular interaction ceases and it becomes super-cooled matter with quite different properties than at room temperature. Molecular interactions cease – but the emission-absorption phenomenon does not! It's still emitting and reabsorbing energy. This is considered the 'zero-point' energy field. But this has been field theory in quantum physics for 40 years! It's a great mystery how this action takes place. Einstein referred to this as 'spooky action at a distance.'"

"A Dyadic Model of Nature"
Conference of Science & Consciousness, April, 1999
(Discussion of Quantum Physics Zero-Point Field)

Zero point field: The empty space found within the universe and in each atom is referred to by physicists as the zero-point field, which exists in space at a constant temperature of -273.15 degrees C or absolute zero. It is also referred to as the "ether" or the "nuether" or the "quantum substrate" or the "sub-quantum matrix." Dr. Carl Jung called it "the realm of universal archetypes" and the "collective unconscious."

In essence, the Quantum Hologram model asserts that there is two-way communication between the zero-point field and all matter through non-local adaptive, resonance. In theory, all matter in the universe, including every human being, has equal instant access to the zero-point field, which if you will, is the cosmic repository of all experience as information.

Quantrek: Quantum Holography

"Free space is not empty. It is a seething caldron of energy."

"A Dyadic Model of Nature"
Conference of Science and Consciousness, April 1999

Quantum Entanglement

"You cannot have choice and determinism simultaneously."

Interview by Carol Mersch
2003

"During recent years I was diagnosed with prostate cancer and kidney cancer because I bought into the idea that as we get older we are subject to disease and aging. I didn't buy into it intellectually, but I bought into it emotionally. And lo and behold, it happened. I was healed by changing my mind."

"A Voyage into Mind and Space,"
Chicago Planetary Studies Foundation, March 2004

Quantum Entanglement

"The profound implications of gaining information from both persons and matter by unconventional means and more particularly of influencing persons and matter by an active process of mind are not adequately addressed . . . unless a scientist was exceedingly courageous and daring, he would not even consider these subjects.

"George, one runs the risk of being very wrong when one sticks his neck out as I am doing. However, I feel very deeply about these observed events whose implications I think are far reaching. I may be wrong—but what if I am *right*."

In a letter to CIA Director George H.W. Bush
as follow-up to a private meeting on remote viewing
December 2, 1976

"Intention is a product of a choice—it's an energy."

Interview by Carol Mersch
2003

"We've stopped burning witches, but we haven't stopped punishing them."

The Way of the Explorer

Mersch: If the process you're describing, resonance and such things, does set energy in motion that changes the balance of things, wouldn't it be true that by reversing a false suggestion or false intention you would affect the outcome?

Mitchell: That is a part of some of what I've written and a part of what Royal Rife, a researcher of years ago, had written, and the notion is that by an anti-wave process, a reverse wave, if you can get a wave characteristic of a disease, you can send the anti-wave, or reverse wave, and it should be therapeutic . . . Just like if we say we can plot a mathematical form of an ocean wave, an anti-wave would be 180 degrees out of phase. If you add those two waves you get a still, flat ocean. It's the same thing with a therapeutic situation. If you can get a frequency phase characteristic associated with a disease or illness or function, then an anti-wave should be therapeutic.

Excerpt of interview on quantum entanglement by Carol Mersch, Lake Worth, FL, October 2003.

Quantum Entanglement

"We often sublimate information and its significance in the subconscious, although it continues to influence our thinking and behaviors."

The Way of the Explorer

The Space Less Traveled

"This is what is factual and known, that free space is not empty, there are quantum fluctuations, there are particles and non-particles popping in and out of existence, disappearing and reappearing. And there is an enormous amount of energy. Some would say there is enough energy in one cubic centimeter of free space to create the entire universe all over again."

"A Dyadic Model of Nature"
Conference of Science & Consciousness
April 1999

Quantum Entanglement

"The classical plutonian notion is that mind does not affect or interact with matter, that you can't do that. Well we know that's just *nonsense!* It does! I'm convinced it works at the quantum level of nature where these resonant interactions take place.

"Whereas incoming information is *perception,* we can call outgoing information *intention.* So my quantum holographic model very nicely models how we get incoming information non-locally in the quantum hologram. It's not quite as simple to model as an intention that has affect out here on inanimate objects. We aren't able to model that as well—or hardly at all—yet."

Interview by Carol Mersch
2003

"Those guys are slightly behind nature, which has
been doing it all along."

In response to a query on a CNN report May 2006
covering the teleporting of quantum information
by leading scientists in Denmark

Quantum Entanglement

"There are [computers] sitting there generating random numbers. But when the collective consciousness focused on something, it threw the random number generators off random. Which shows us there *isn't* such a thing as randomness, in general."

Interview by Carol Mersch
2003

"Dr. Dean Radin's work out of my institute involved Dr. Robert Jahn's work at Princeton, showing that *intention* and *attention* are related. They have shown that attention affects Random Number Generators (RNGs); and it is now well established statistically. Radin's work is showing that with major collective events, such as 9/11 where he had a series of RNGs set up, the 9/11 event caused the world's network of RNGs to go off random."

Interview by Carol Mersch
2003

Quantum Entanglement

"When we talk about *perception*, some people would not recognize that. But the more sensitive you are, the more you will pick that up. The more you're resonating at the non local quantum level—what I write about as quantum holography—you're resonating at a non-local level and you're resonating at this level of interaction. The obvious is among parents and children and between lovers when you're in sync. Or athletes when they're in 'the zone,' as they say. You're operating in this resonant condition—where the system is operating as one, as opposed to various individuals. And that's a quantum phenomenon."

Interview by Carol Mersch
2003

"I don't believe in luck. What people call luck are random occurrences."

Interview by Carol Mersch
2003

Quantum Entanglement

Question: *Are there any negative consequences of the interconnectedness of matter?*

"There may be negative consequences of the interconnectedness of matter, but I haven't thought about it because there have been so many negative consequences of considering ourselves separate."

Lecture at Whitehouse High School, Germantown, TN
January 25, 2005
(In response to question from an honor student)

EXTRATERRESTRIAL

Extraterrestrial

"When we go to Mars—and we will in due course—and we look back at this tiny little planet from which we came, it's going to sound rather foolish to say, 'I came from the United States,' or 'I came from France,' or from Russia, or Israel, or China. No, we will say, 'I came from planet Earth.'"

"A Voyage into Mind and Space"
Chicago Planetary Studies Foundation, March 2004

"We are not alone in the universe. This world is too strange, too magnificent, too wonderful for us to inhabit it alone."

The Geraldo Show
1986

Extraterrestrial

"I have often been asked if we carried weapons to the moon in the event extraterrestrials were there first. I reply that if they were there first, they would be more advanced than we, thus we wouldn't need them."

When Foxes Guard the Henhouse

"Given that there are billions of solar systems and galaxies, and around those solar systems there are likely billions of planets with life bearing probability, there is almost zero probability that we are alone in the universe. And it is also almost zero probability that we are the most advanced civilization in the universe."

Lecture at Whitehouse High School, Germantown, TN
January 25, 2005

"Our technology is not nearly as sophisticated as theirs. It's pretty obvious that had they been hostile, we would be gone by now."

The Daily Telegraph, July 24, 2008
(Regarding Aliens)

The Space Less Traveled

The Geraldo Show, 1986 (when asked about hard evidence of UFOs on the moon):

Mitchell: As far as I know there is no smoking gun evidence in the public domain. . .

Tim Crawford, Founder, UFO Central: But the NASA data from the probes that we've sent to both Mars and to the Moon show photographic evidence of ancient ruins both on Mars and the Moon.

Mitchell: I've looked at that and it's just not there. I'm sorry, you're dead wrong. You're perpetuating a hoax on people. And you're dead wrong

Crawford: . . . Does that suggest that one individual can shoot down the data of an entire community of people? The information is on video for the entire world to see and it's academically presented! With all due respect, I find that . . .

Geraldo: But he was there! He walked on it!

Mitchell: Wait a minute! Wait a minute! Part of this came from *my* mission site! And it's suggested that the reflection of the ruins came from *my* visor. And that *is simply not true*!

The Space Less Traveled

"Yes, we've been visited. I've been deeply involved in certain committees and certain research programs with very credible scientists and research people that have the inside story. I've been privileged to work with military centers and intelligence centers that have been briefed in knowledge beneath the surface of what has been public knowledge.

"There's more nonsense out there about this than there is real knowledge. But it is a real phenomenon. It's been well covered up by our governments for the past sixty years."

Kerrang! Radio
July 23, 2008

"In the briefing of the Joint Chiefs of Staff
Intelligence Group, it became very clear that they
were naive. They did not really know any more
about this effort than we do, if as much. That is
because...most of the people in government were
not in government when I retired twenty-five years
ago, they are younger people. The files going back
fifty years just no longer exist. . . And in my own
efforts in talking with these folks, and talking with
government, the question often comes up as to
how they could have kept this a secret for so long.
It's been around us all the time, but it has been
denied and obscured.

"I often like to state the condition—the myth, if
you will—about Columbus coming here and some
of the Indians not seeing the ships simply because
it was not in their collective consciousness or their
repertoire. They, at least, did not want to see them.
Much of what we're seeing now is what many
people do not want to see either. There has been a

(continued)

massive effort at creating a mindset of denying the obvious, of saying that you're not seeing what's sitting right in front of you right now, thus causing doubt in your own mind. It's amazingly effective.

"So documentation and evidence that is probably the smoking gun type of evidence has been totally compromised by saying that it's simply not true . . . They haven't kept the secret, but it has been totally compromised by misinformation and disinformation."

Exopolitics Conference
National Press Club, Washington DC, April 2009

Extraterrestrial

"I don't know how or where or when they're doing it, but they've been observing us here for quite some time. I believe what I'm saying and I cite the evidence that I know.

"The reason for the denial is, number one, they didn't know if these were hostile and if we could protect ourselves from them. And, two, didn't want to Soviets to know. So they devised to lie about it and cover it up.

"We've got billions and billions of stars in the galaxy, and billions and billions of galaxies. It doesn't take but a few planets around a few stars to have quite a few civilizations."

Interview by Tim Malloy, 5HD-WPTV
Lake Worth, FL, November 9, 2010

Rob Sidon: *Personally, I've never given much heed to UFOs, except in science fiction, particularly with all the hoaxes. . . But the notion of universal consciousness seems entirely intuitive to me. The advance of exopolitics seems logical and beneficial. Exopolitics is the discipline of studying relations between our human civilization and other intelligent civilizations in the universe.*

Edgar Mitchell: And included in exopolitics is the notion of being in league with them. In other words, having a connection with them and seeing what we can learn. And are they with us? Are we in danger on this? I think the consensus is that the visitors—if they wish us harm—would have done it a long time ago. But they haven't. There seems to be more evidence for their wanting to observe and to assist our evolution than to destroy us in any way.

Note: Information concerning extraterrestrial life and technology is kept secret from the general public, elected
(continued)

political representatives, and even senior military officials.

The supporting evidence is overwhelming in scope and shows that decision making is restricted on a strict 'need to know' basis. [Source: Expolitics.org]

Interview by Rob Sidon
Common Ground, May 2012

The Space Less Traveled

Dr. Edgar Mitchell on Larry King Live
CNN: *UFO Cover-up? Or Not?* July 12, 2008

Larry King: We are now joined by a distinguished American in West Palm Beach, the Apollo 14 astronaut Edgar Mitchell, the sixth man to walk on the moon. Many of the Roswell witnesses told Dr. Mitchell their account, which he says were later verified by a contact at the Pentagon. What do you believe, Dr. Mitchell?

Mitchell: I happened to have lived in the area and I grew up in the area. My family had farming and ranch holdings and farm machinery holdings. We knew many of the people, including the ranch where this was discovered; and in spite of all their security oaths, the talk in the community was that it was an alien craft—and those stories survived all of the other stories.

And because of who I was, and what I was, and

(*continued*)

because I lived in the area and grew up in the area, and because I was an astronaut, some of them wanted to get it off their chest before they passed on. All of them were under very severe oaths and fear and penalty for talking, but they did want to talk.

I eventually went to the Pentagon and asked for a meeting with the intelligence committee of the Joint Chiefs of Staff...He called a few weeks later and said he had found the source of the Black Budget funding for this project and that he was going to subsequently investigate.

We did get a call some time later, and a report much later than that, saying that he had found the people responsible for the cover-up and was told: "I'm sorry, Admiral, you do not have a need to know."

Skeptic Bill Nye: Yeah, but they were not on their death bed. A death bed declaration is quite a different thing than seeking you and telling their story. *(continued)*

Mitchell: I am not interested in arguing with you. I'm telling my story. If you want to shut up and hear it I'll be glad to talk.

THE UNIVERSE

"Everything in the universe is part of the same whole and a derivative of the same original source, therefore it is interconnected. And what one does to others, one does to one's self."

Interview by Carol Mersch
2003

"There's as many galaxies in the universe as there are stars in the Milky Way.

"Our galaxy is 100,000 light years in diameter, and it is only one of hundreds of billions of galaxies. The Milky Way galaxy contains approximately 200 to 400 billion stars. The nearest galaxy, which is our own Andromeda, is 2.2 million light years away, a light year being 5.9 trillion years.

"We hadn't heard about trillions until we started reading about the current federal budget."

"Understanding the Functions and Power of the Quantum Hologram," IONS 2009

"It's instant global consciousness. You become aware of it when you're in space.

"For me it was the experience of recognizing that we are part of the process of the universe. And we are one with the universe. That it's a holistic and intelligent universe.

"That whole idea about who we are, where we came from, how we got here, and where we're going, is really being revised as a result of modern science, space travel, and from viewing ourselves from a totally different perspective. And it has enormous implications for what we humans really are, what our future is, and what our destiny is."

The Geraldo Show, 1986
Commentary on his space experience

The Universe

"It is our destiny to go outside our solar system before the century is over and to continue to explore and expand into the universe. Whether we will do it in this hundred years depends on whether we survive this hundred years. And we are in danger of not doing that."

"A Voyage into Mind and Space"
Chicago Planetary Studies Foundation, March 2004

"To me, divinity is the intelligence existing in the universe. That universe is a learning, growing, changing organism, like the human beings who strive to understand it, and who have only begun to explore it."

The Way of the Explorer

"We went into space as technologists. We came back as humanists."

The Geraldo Show
1996

"The story of ourselves as created from a scientific cosmology is incomplete and possibly flawed. And the story of ourselves as created by our cultural cosmologies is archaic and most certainly flawed."

Lecture at Whitehouse High School, Germantown, TN
January 2005

'Buckminster Fuller once said, 'If you want to understand the human condition, you must first understand the universe.'

"But if you want to understand that universe, you must first understand yourself."

"Heroes and Healers"
November 2002

"I believe in the divine nature of the universe in that my definition of Deity may be a little different than most people. I believe the universe is a self-organizing, intelligent, creative, learning, trial and error, participatory, integrative, evolving system. And those attributes are precisely the attributes that ancients gave to Deity."

Lecture at Whitehouse High School, Germantown, TN
January 2005

Insight

The sky's all aglow, rare gases, slow flow
Form worlds in the fullness of time.
Stars spin in their flight, tiny points of light
Beam life into Nature's glad rhyme.

My mind fills with awe, comprehends what it saw
Spirit yearns to fathom the plan
How movement so fine and each tiny line
Ties one to the other to man.

The light the eye sees from each stately tree,
But a pattern of energy whirling,
As atoms that spin, disappear now and then
But emerge to show nature unfurling.

It's all part of One, a song that is sung
Each note at its place in the tune
In this universe wide, each segment is tied,
The earth to the stars to the moon.

A tapestry bold in bright hues with gold,
Each thread a part of the story.

The Space Less Traveled

The tiniest mite, a star large and bright,
Together must share their glory.

Thought arose from this mass, at some age now
past,
To bring purpose and will to the plan
Of God manifest, of species all blessed,
Together in peace on the land.

From a collection of poems by Edgar Mitchell

"We are in the process of convincing ourselves that the limitations of special relativity, the predictions of general relativity, and the interpretations of early quantum theory are not absolute, but rather stepping stones to a new understanding of the cosmos and how to explore it. It is the human destiny to explore our world.

"We may use robots to lead the way, but we will not feel that we have fulfilled destiny until we make it a personal journey. And to do so, we must break the light barrier both in propulsion and communications technologies. My article of faith is that we shall be able to do so in the coming decades.

"So, 'Beam me somewhere, Scotty!'"

"Space Flight as an Anticipatory Computing System"
Institute of Noetic Sciences, 2000

In Closing

"Until the day presidents and prime ministers around the globe propose a mandate stating that humankind will make that next giant leap, we will dream and continue to make modest forays into the near heavens. A more ambitious day will inevitably come.

"Perhaps it will be our children or grandchildren, or even their children, but one day a craft from this shimmering blue dot will lower into a pale red Martian horizon. Then, gradually, imperceptibly, but inevitably, the shimmering blue dot will slowly recede in the view of the spacecraft that will carry our children's children throughout the ghostly white of the Milky Way.

"Still others will follow, and with them the ancient stories of their predecessors. Then they will leave the galaxy in order to make themselves in the image of God."

Edgar Mitchell
The Way of the Explorer

Apollo 14 Astronaut
Navy Captain Dr. Edgar D. Mitchell

About the Author

Apollo 14 astronaut Edgar Mitchell is one of only twelve men who rode a Saturn rocket all the way to the moon. On February 5, 1971, Navy Capt. Dr. Edgar Mitchell became the sixth man to walk on its surface.

On March 1, 1971, he was awarded the Presidential Medal of Freedom by President Richard M. Nixon and was subsequently instrumental in founding the Association of Space Explorers, an organization of astronauts from around the world who have flown in space, formed "to encourage international cooperation in the exploration of science and space and to foster greater environmental awareness."

He left NASA in 1973 to found the Institute of Noetic Sciences, a worldwide organization dedicated to the research of global awareness and universal consciousness. In October 1997, he was inducted into the Astronaut Hall of Fame In honor of his contribution to the study of universal awareness and global sustainability, in 2005 Mitchell was nominated for the Nobel Peace Prize.

In 2011 he received the da Vinci Award for societal advancement through research and understanding of human consciousness and psyche.

Scientist, test pilot, naval officer, astronaut, entrepreneur, author, and lecturer, Dr. Mitchell's career personifies humankind's eternal thrust to widen its horizons through the exploration of inner and outer space.

About Carol Mersch

Carol Mersch is an Oklahoma businesswoman and author of *The Apostles of Apollo*, a chronicle of the little-known voyage of the Bible to the surface of the moon during the Apollo era. It was the culmination of a project that consumed five years of her life.

Mersch's journey began years ago when she heard Edgar Mitchell speak at a business conference in Orlando. He stood at a podium, regaling the audience with the technical tales of his mission and the one that preceded it—the ill-fated Apollo 13. Mitchell gave the ultimate insider's view of the unfolding drama that ultimately brought the crew back alive. He ended with the summation: "After all was said and done, I'm convinced it was the power of thousands of praying minds that pulled that spacecraft back into earth orbit." With that, he thanked the audience and left the stage.

For the next fifteen years these words were never far from Mersch's mind as she wondered what he meant and why he said them. In 2003 she tracked

him down and landed a breakfast conversation with him in Palm Beach, Florida, during which he took the time to elaborate on his theories concerning the nature of awareness, quantum physics, and the interconnectedness of life.

The meeting initiated a years-long dialogue. Mitchell granted hours of interviews and access to his archives, during which time she learned that Mitchell had landed the first Bible on the moon. Their paths crossed many times in the coming years as Mersch tracked and documented the twists and turns of Mitchell's public and private life, amassing a formidable library of dialog from his media appearances, lectures, articles, books, and everyday conversations.

The Space Less Traveled represents a cross-section of literary excerpts gleaned from this collection which Mersch believes offers a rich cornucopia of all things wise—and all things Mitchell.

Also by C.L. Mersch: *The Apostles of Apollo.*

Legend of Sources

Albuquerque Journal, March 30, 1971

Common Ground, "Edgar Dean Mitchell: An American Astronaut's Tireless Trek," May 2012, interview by Rob Sidon

The Daily Telegraph, July 4, 2008

"A Dyadic Model of Nature," Conference of Science & Consciousness discussion of Quantum Physics' Zero Point Field, April 1999

For All Mankind, Harry Hurt III, The Atlantic Monthly Press, NY, 1988

"The Future of Healing," WLRN-TV, October 10, 2001

The Geraldo Show, 1972.

"Go Forth and Sustain the World: The 21st (century) Commandment," a parody on sustainability, talk delivered by Mitchell in 1996

"Heroes and Healers," panel discussion, Nov. 2002

Interview by Carol Mersch, Lake Worth, FL, 2003

Interview by Carol Mersch, Lake Worth, FL, 2005

Interview by Carol Mersch, Dallas, TX, 2006

Interview with *Kerrang! Radio*, July 23, 2008

Interview with Tim Malloy, 5HD-WPTV, regarding alien visitors, November 9, 2010

Institute of Noetic Science (IONS) summary report, October 23, 2008

Larry King Live, "UFO Cover-up? Or Not?" July 17, 2008

Lecture, IONS Group, Convention Center, Germantown, TN, January 2005

Lecture, Unity Church, Germantown, TN, January 2005

Lecture atWhitehouse High School, Germantown, TN, January 2005

Lecture, Unity Church, Dallas, TX, 2006

Letter to Apollo 15 astronaut James Irwin, August 23, 1978

Letter to CIA Director George H. W. Bush, December 1, 1976

The Monthly Aspectarian, Morton Grove, IL, November, 2001

"My Vision for the Third Millennium," paper by Edgar Mitchell

Poems by Edgar D. Mitchell (written in early 1980s): "Essence" "Insight " "Love Means Letting go of Fear," with acknow-ledgement to Jerry Jampolski "Muffy's Graduation" "Musings of a Father" "The Roué's Downfall" "Search"

Psychic Exploration, Dr. Edgar D. Mitchell, Cosimo Books, NY, 1974, 2011

"Quantrek: Quantum Holography" brochure, Edgar Mitchell

Sadhguru, Tucson, AZ, June 2009

San Francisco Chronicle, September 16, 2007

Spacefest Conference, Phoenix, AZ, 2007

The Sunday Brand, Hereford, TX, September 2, 1971

"Thoughts on World Peace," Universal Peace Conference, 1983

"Toward a Sustainable Global Future," Lecture, IONS 2009

UACC Conference, San Antonio, TX, August 2006

"Understanding the Functions and Power of the Quantum Hologram," IONS, 2009

"The View from Space," Edgar D. Mitchell (DVD), SMPI, January 2005

"Voices for Sustainability," documentary, *Living Dreams Films*, 2010

"A Voyage into Mind and Space" Lecture, Chicago Planetary Studies Foundation, Marcy 2004

The Way of the Explorer, Edgar Mitchell with Dwight Williams

When Foxes Guard the Hen House, unpublished manuscript by Drs. Edgar D. Mitchell and Carol Rosin, 1987

Made in the USA
Lexington, KY
17 February 2013